AF416689

Contents

All Scripture is taken from the New American Standard Bible, 1995.

July 4, 2020

Introduction to the Concept of Sacrifice

Overview

The Lexham Theological Workbook (LTW) defines the word *sacrifice* as "The act of offering something as a means of atonement, worship, or thanksgiving. The offering may involve slaughtering an animal or making an offering of grain or another agricultural product."[1] However, this definition may not be adequate in consideration of a synthesis of both Old and New Testament exegesis. With that in mind, the purpose of this paper will be to outline and evaluate the historical and theological structure in which the concept of *sacrifice* originates and then prove a proper expositional framework in which to understand the New Testament death of Jesus Christ.

A Definition of Sacrifice

As mentioned above, the LTW gives the scholar a basic conceptual understanding of what occurs in the act of sacrifice. This concept is shared among many theological dictionaries, and is certainly within the boundary of orthodoxy, though not robust in its detail. The Oxford Dictionary of the Christian Church (OXDCC) additionally indicates specific earmarks of sacrifice, namely, indicating to whom the act directed, and that the sacrifice must genuinely be one of value or cost;[2] this will be a useful point in the work of understanding what a sacrifice is and should accomplish, as this is one of the earliest understandings given to us in the biblical record.

---

[1] Lesley Difransico, "Sacrifice," ed. Douglas Mangum et al., *Lexham Theological Wordbook*, Lexham Bible Reference Series (Bellingham, WA: Lexham Press, 2014).

[2] F. L. Cross and Elizabeth A. Livingstone, eds., The Oxford Dictionary of the Christian Church (Oxford; New York: Oxford University Press, 2005), 1447.

In the book of Genesis, the concept of sacrifice occurs early. The brothers Cain, and Abel, are recorded as giving sacrifice to God in chapter four, verses three through seven—a passage which will consequently give us more insight into a working understanding of sacrifice. A critical point of exegesis in this text points to the Hebrew word, שעה, in verse five, in which the Bible tells the reader that God had "no regard" to the offering of Cain. The perfect tense verb given here has no regard to the time or process of investigating the nature of the offering but rather indicates that God does not even extend consideration to the offering, because of the one offering it.

Derek Kidner further emphasizes the point in his commentary on Genesis. He notes that the only explicit understanding of the nature of the sacrifice that a reader should take away from this passage is that Cain's spirit was arrogant.[3] This arrogance clarifies for the reader, why God would reject considering Cain's offering, as the New Testament book of James, explicitly tells the Christian that God rebuffs the proud, instead choosing to draw near to the humble (Jas 4:6).

Considering these things, we can, from the outset, take away that initial definition presented from the LTW is, as discussed, not robust enough to move forward with, especially as this paper dives further into linking this act with the sacrificial death of Jesus Christ.

The Difference Between Sacrifice and Ritual

Having a broadened understanding of earmarks of biblical sacrifice, we can now consider this against an understanding of ritual, as some have previously considered that *ritual* is a better theoretical term under which to discuss the topic.

---

[3]   Derek Kidner, Genesis: An Introduction and Commentary, vol. 1, Tyndale Old Testament Commentaries (Downers Grove, IL: InterVarsity Press, 1967), 80.

James W. Watts critiques the writings of Martin Modéus, who wrote on the ritual perspective of biblical sacrifice. He notes Modéus' theory that the term *ritual* calls attention to the *cause* of the activity, rather than the sheer action itself,[4] which is a reasonable argument from Modéus.

The argument is further defended by Modéus, saying, "they define the nature of a *causa* in order to clarify a situation of transition, ambiguity, or conflict.[5]

To this point, we have only evaluated Genesis four, where Cain and Abel act, by giving a sacrifice to God. However, we can certainly evaluate the understanding of a sacrifice vs. a ritual within the confines of this early activity.

In defining *sacrifice* there is undoubtedly some act of worship that is or is not, enacted. That Cain experiences rejection for his arrogance, strongly evidences that the act of sacrifice itself was not what was acceptable but rather, in the confines of the term *worship,* some crucial ingredient was missing, assumed to be humility. So now, we must focus on what the source of that humility ought to be.

---

[4] James W. Watts, "Review of Sacrifice and Symbol: Biblical Šĕlāmîm in a Ritual Perspective by Modéus, Martin." Review of Biblical Literature (2006).

[5] Ibid.

Looking back, we remember the story of Cain's parents, Adam, and Eve, fallen in to sin in the garden of Eden. Tricked by Satan, in the form of a Serpent, the newly forged couple fell into grasping at that which was not only not given to them, but explicitly denied to them, by God. God allowed them to both physically live, but with a punishment—however, these punishments were also lessened in some senses, as God provided a covering to the fallen man and woman, promising a Savior to undo the act that occurred in Eden. This act of mercy should have elicited humility in Adam, Eve, and all who would presumably hear after that day.

It is then fair to understand that *sacrifice*, as in the definition provided, may not fully develop the concept of an *internal loyalty* rather than just an act interpreted in whatever way one is inclined to do so.

This misunderstanding is perhaps the reason for the confusion in understanding why Cain's sacrifice suffered rejection. The most natural conclusion to make regarding Cain's rejection in the Genesis account is that what he gave as a sacrifice was inadequate as a means of worship—this is a common understanding considering standard definitions of sacrifice. However, further study reveals that, as discussed, God discounted his sacrifice, not because of type, but because of spiritual condition. That spiritual condition, should emanate from a thankfulness born of the mercy God showed on humanity at the fall, as this is the only historical narrative we have before the pericope in question. Now, this may be splitting hairs, or a subtle point not worth the time and effort of a theological paper, however, we must remember that many heresies build from subtle misunderstandings (intentional or not) of complex theological issues.

In comparing the idea of *ritual*, as Modéus does, he focuses in on the word *šelāmîm*, which has its uses majorly in priestly cultic context[6] but also appears in biblical language. Number 6:14 is an exciting look into its use. The English word *offering* is used four times in this verse alone. A different underlying Hebrew word accompanies each use of the word. This phenomenon is accounted for in English, using adjectives modifying the term *sacrifice* in each instance (i.e., burnt, sin, and peace). The Hebrew, however, has different terminology for each instance, and the Hebrew use of *šelāmîm,* meaning *peace offering*, indicates the existence of a breach between parties, resulting in significant debt.

What is not clarified by Modéus in his explanation is why *šelāmîm* receives more focus than the other words. Modéus does give a beginning analysis of why, but, as Watts notes, his words require more explanation. In evaluating, Watts acknowledges the words of Modéus that, "in particular, his argument that life situations (*causae*) carry the weight of meaning while ritual symbols serve to define, legitimize, or mark the significance of these situations is a valuable contribution to ritual studies quite separate from its application to biblical texts."[7]

---

[6]   T. Seidl, "שְׁלָמִים," ed. G. Johannes Botterweck, Helmer Ringgren, and Heinz-Josef Fabry, trans. David E. Green, Theological Dictionary of the Old Testament (Grand Rapids, MI; Cambridge, U.K.: William B. Eerdmans Publishing Company, 2006), 115.

[7]   James W. Watts, "Review of Sacrifice and Symbol: Biblical Šĕlāmîm in a Ritual Perspective by Modéus, Martin." Review of Biblical Literature (2006).

Watts explains that this idea of Modéus is born from the tendencies of humanity to mark specific life occurrences with individual *ritualistic acts*, which is correct. We should look no further than the Genesis account of the fall, in which God ritualistically marks the promise to crush the head of the serpent, by covering Adam and Eve in the animal skins—an action very close in nature to the concept of biblical sacrifice itself.

Perhaps what the reader/scholar should begin to consider is that this is not an "either/or" issue and that there may be merit in constructing a concept of sacrifice from both, the sacrificial terms usually spoken of by Christians and the ritualistic terms that Modéus seems to prefer. Further research into the biblical use of the concept of sacrifice will be required to determine this.

Biblical Concepts of Sacrifice

Overview

If clarification is essential to the concept, and the definition of *sacrifice*, research into how the term exists in Scripture will be necessary. The research is no easy task, as already noted.

A single verse (Num 6:14) uses four different Hebrew terms to describe parts of the sacrificial system. Nevertheless, both the pre-law and post-law Old Testament (PR/PT OT, respectively) necessitate evaluation, to see how far early concepts of sacrifice mirror Modéus' idea of ritual, and to see if PTOT was in any way changed or is potentially affected by outside influences.

The Use of Sacrifice in the Bible

Pre-Law Uses of Sacrifice

PROT uses of sacrifice have already been evaluated, to some degree, in the historical context of Cain and Abel. However, there is another compelling story that should bear significant weight on the discussion: Abraham's sacrifice of Isaac in Genesis 22.

Abraham Oh of Chongshin University and Seminary, in the Republic of Korea, has written a prolific piece regarding the Aqedah (AQ), which is an alleged theology in the Jewish tradition regarding the sacrifice of Isaac (SI), coupled with concepts of atonement.[8] Oh posits that this theory is unproven in the New Testament (NT).

However, it is a prominent theology in Jewish circles, speaking directly into if this influenced the OT persons before the law. This is so, first, because it is suggested that the SI from the Genesis story is a pre-configuration of what is called a cultic system in Leviticus, and thus the Historical books,[9] and second, because there may be a conscious connection to NT theology.

Looking into the Genesis account, the reader encounters Abraham, who has been given a promise by God, sealed in a ritual vow (Gen 15), in which God has told him he would both be given a son and a nation from that Son. The AQ would have its reader understand this story with the emphasis that the SI would not only be a model of sacrifice going forward but that the SI itself would even build the framework of the atoning work of Jesus Christ.

---

[8] Abraham Oh, "Canonical understanding of the sacrifice of Isaac: The influence of the Jewish tradition." HTS Teologiese Studies 72, no. 3 (2016): 1+. Gale Academic OneFile (accessed May 23, 2020).

[9] Ibid.

Oh rightly criticizes this as outmoded, first because Isaac did not die in the story recorded in Genesis, though some Jewish literature has suggested he did bleed for a short period, as Abraham may have begun the process of sacrifice. Second, the AQ also is attached to concepts of salvation and eternal life. The concepts are certainly inadequate and unfamiliar to NT theology, or OT concepts of sacrifice. God has indicated in the covering of Adam and Eve, the sacrifice provided was insufficient to atone for the broken covenant. Nevertheless, while covering was provided in the immediate, a Savior was promised for permanency.

The promises provided to Abraham from God were theoretically agreed to by both sides. However, in the anesthetizing of Abraham, God takes up both sides of the commitment and lays the burden to keep the promise totally on Himself (Heb 6:13-14), and so in practice does not technically require the obedience of Abraham to fulfill the promises—this is a mark sorely missed in the AQ understanding of the SI. However, this draws us back to Genesis 22. One of the standard notations of this passage is difficulty in balancing the promise God gives, with the requirement for Abraham's obedience in God's "testing" of him. The requirement of Abraham to pass this test was not tongue-in-cheek by God, but instead using His typical method of employing and arresting men's will to His purposes.

What is interesting is the glaring omission in suggesting the AQ here. While proponents of the position would look to promulgate this as a paradigm for the Levitical system, what is paradigmatic (and not emphasized enough by Oh in response to this) is that the structure of Abraham's call to sacrifice Isaac calls immediate attention to the willingness of Abraham's heart to obey his God. In fact, Oh highlights that the AQ proponents believe that Isaac was active and willing in his cooperation with the endeavor, but it indescribable as paradigmatic in the way that the process itself plays out.

Combining these thoughts, what we can take away from PROT uses of sacrifice is that emphasis lies heavily upon the infraction for which it is required (as noted by Modéus in his concept of ritual), and upon the conscious spirit and attitude behind the action (as noted in the review of Cain and Abel's sacrifice). As of now, the actual act of sacrifice (that is, the process performed) has not proven to be as critical as the other pieces. We will see if this holds, as we investigate PTOT uses of sacrifice, and if *the object* sacrificed will eventually play a part as well.

Post-Law Old Testament Uses of Sacrifice

It is here wise to note that there is a common three-fold understanding of the law referenced in the OT by Christian scholars: The Ethical Law, the Civil Law, and the Ceremonial Law. Exodus 20 and on divulges, formally, both the Ethical Law and the Civil Law to the newly freed Israelites. Exodus 24:8 sees the ratification of that covenant, different from the memory of Abraham's covenant, in which God here does require the faithfulness of the Israelite people, and their fidelity; "God's covenant people are required to pledge themselves to the acceptance of the terms of the King."[10]

---

[10]   Iain D. Campbell, *Opening up Exodus*, Opening Up Commentary (Leominster: Day One Publications, 2006), 95.

In doing so, the Sacrificial system enacted in Leviticus would illustrate itself to be connected to, as Modéus described, acts that indicate the nature of the commitment. "Marking symbols focus on and draw attention to the *causa*. Though meaningless by themselves, marking symbols differentiate the ritual from normal life."[11] In describing the different sacrifices (i.e., burn, sin, peace), God differentiates typical life from these acts of sacrifice that indicate something outside of normal circumstances have occurred; that something is a violation of the mutually agreed upon covenant commitment.

This structure is different from PROT in that God had not commanded the nature of the object of sacrifice, but first focused on the attitude of the practice. Now, God will predominantly demand the nature of the sacrifice be addressed but has built into this provision for those unable to comply with the law, which again points back to the sincere desire of God, that man's heart is given to worship Him.

Misunderstandings of Sacrifice

The easiest misunderstandings come from the previous pages of this paper. One of the most common misunderstandings is that what was provided by Cain was wrong. This confusion is mostly inferred through further reading of the Pentateuch because God instituted specific animals for specific sins and sacrifices.

It is easy to see, through a detailed reading of Leviticus, that God specifies sacrifice and all its elements, but it is a better position to realize that God would later say that the blood of bulls and goats was never what was necessary.

---

[11] James W. Watts, "Review of Sacrifice and Symbol: Biblical Šĕlāmîm in a Ritual Perspective by Modéus, Martin," *Review of Biblical Literature* (2006).

Preferably, God wanted contrite and broken hearts, love of mercy and justice, and a faithful commitment to Him as the heart of sacrifice, which alludes back to our earlier discussion of the resolute offering of Abel against the backdrop of Cain's arrogance and thanklessness of the mercy of God. The act was useless, without the proper spirit, and the proper spirit pointed to the ultimate requirements God desires.

It is here also wise to indicate that God also had provision for those who would afford the required animals for specific offerings; this again shows us the heart and desire of God. It was obedience that failed in the garden, and it would be obedience that God would still demand in all that followed that fall.

It is here we will keep these things near our minds, as we dive into the Prophetic understanding of sacrifice in the Scriptures, and how the Jewish people would understand sacrifice in the prophetic era, and moving into the New Testament.

Prophecy and Sacrifice

Overview

Considering the Prophets view is not an easy task, because there are not many instances in which we can review sacrifice use that is different from the law already established. Genesis instances and Levitical law have laid down the blueprint for the system, and despite Israel becoming lethargic in its spiritual application of it, they did generally follow the principle, and the days of atonement and other significant sacrificial calendar days were in line with the law given.

What did the Prophets Believe?

The prophet Jonah does, however, present us with a fascinating opportunity to examine another use of the word translated *sacrifice*. In the first chapter of Jonah, the prophet is in flight from God, and in his abdication of duty, he takes leave on a ship, foolishly, away from God and his calling. God causes a storm on the waters while Jonah is fast asleep. The men of the ship wake him, and they all begin (except for Jonah) to become troubled and call out to their gods, in the hope of mercy. Jonah eventually admits he is on the run from God and offers himself up to be thrown in the water to save the rest of the people on the boat.

Had proponents of the AQ acknowledged a passage such this, they would make a more durable case for their position, because Jonah put himself in a position of anticipated death and he follows through with the act; it was only a miracle of God that preserved him. Jonah here sacrifices himself for the life of the crew, to keep them all from perishing. This willing act of completed sacrifice is closer to what the AQ concept than the SI, but it is still inadequate for comparison, for reasons to be explained later in this offering.

Noteworthy here, though, is that the remainder of the crew responded, in that they began to "fear the Lord greatly" (Jon 1:16). The Scripture records that they offered a *sacrifice* (זֶבַח) to the Lord, *made vows*. Again, the connection of the genuine internal reverence for God is associated with the activity of sacrifice. Douglas Stuart comments on this verse, saying, "It does not seem to describe anything that the sailors did immediately after the storm stopped, but rather relates to the audience the fact that the events the sailors had witnessed were so awesome as to have made a profound and lasting impression on them."[12] This lasting impression of awe was something that dissipated for the Jews over time.

---

[12] Douglas Stuart, *Hosea–Jonah*, vol. 31, Word Biblical Commentary (Dallas: Word, Incorporated, 1987), 464.

What did the Jews believe?

The Jewish response to the ongoing requirement and concept of sacrifice entirely misses the point. God did not find worth in their sacrifices (though they thought to continue God's ordained sacrifices while also sacrificing to false gods was acceptable), but instead says this in Jeremiah 7:

22   "For I did not speak to your fathers, or command them in the day that I brought them out of the land of Egypt, concerning burnt offerings and sacrifices.

23   "But this is what I commanded them, saying, 'Obey My voice, and I will be your God, and you will be My people; and you will walk in all the way which I command you, that it may be well with you.'[13]

What God desired from His people was obedience. R.K. Harrison says, "Here Jeremiah is not repudiating the value of sacrifice as such, but is denouncing the wicked and apostate who have made the rituals an end in themselves and have thus abused the cultic forms.[14] In time, the Jews moved beyond these basic requirements.

The NT Jew was little different from the PTOT Jew in that they had become apathetic to loving God and being in awe of Him and recalling His great deeds on their behalf. The overarching concept of *sacrifice* and *ritual* share many components and seem best used together to build on the demands of God from His people. We will next look at the death of Jesus and see if this understanding is fitting and more robust to describe the work of Christ.

---

[13]   *New American Standard Bible: 1995 Update* (La Habra, CA: The Lockman Foundation, 1995), Je 7:22–23.

[14]   R. K. Harrison, *Jeremiah and Lamentations: An Introduction and Commentary*, vol. 21, Tyndale Old Testament Commentaries (Downers Grove, IL: InterVarsity Press, 1973), 90.

The Death of Jesus Christ

Overview

A dramatic change in the NT view of sacrifice, post-death of Jesus, and the later destruction of the temple in AD 70. Ullucci notes, "Julian's *Against the Galileans* noted that Christians, in rejecting animal sacrifices, are going against what their own scriptures mandate, 'for Abraham used to sacrifice all the time just as we [Hellenes] do."[15] This significant change from the OT processes of *sacrifice* bucks at the simplistic definition imposed upon the word by the LTW. Experiencing the death of Christ, the Jewish Christians moved from their understanding of animal sacrifice and understood the true meaning behind it—devotion to God.

Theories on the Atonement

There are several theories on the atonement, and Millard Erickson cites a handful in his *Christian Theology* book (CT). He notates the Socinian theory, in which Christ is merely an example. The Moral-Influence theory depicts the sacrifice and atonement of Christ as a demonstration of God's love, showing Christ's divine dimensions.

The Governmental theory which emphasizes sin, and atonement satisfies demands of justice detached from the occurrence, and Christ's death is a warning against sin.

The Ransom theory is a popular theory in which God and Satan battle in a cosmic duel over the outcome of humankind. In Ransom Theory, God must pay ransom to Satan for the price of sin. Lastly, Satisfaction theory, in which God satisfies the demands of justice, which are core to the nature of God. The payment is owed to God, and so the perfect Son is given to pay that price.[16]

---

[15] O'Leary, Joseph. "Five Books on Sacrifice: New Approaches in Sacrifice Studies." Reviews in religion and theology 21, no. 3 (July 2014).

The Lexham Survey of Theology (LST) adds in Christus Victor theory in which the death of Christ is a cosmic victory over an unknown being. The Scapegoat Theory is reminiscent of other theories, but here Christ appears as the scapegoat (the Azazel) of Leviticus 16 and accepts the consequences of sin on itself, with no debt payment to anyone. Additionally, the penal substitution, in which God is just and the justifier of the sinner, allows Christ to take on the debt of sin, and receive the due punishment for it, exchanging His righteousness for our sin.[17]

Correctly Applying the Concept of Sacrifice to the Cross

Overview

Now understanding concepts of standard definitions of *sacrifice*, *ritual*, and having some sense of different understandings on the theories of Christ's atonement, we ask the question, "how can we properly understand the work of Christ?"

---

[16]   Millard J. Erickson, Christian Theology, 3rd ed. (Grand Rapids, MI: Baker Academic, 2013), 727.

[17]   Mark Olivero, "Theories of Atonement," in Lexham Survey of Theology, ed. Mark Ward et al. (Bellingham, WA: Lexham Press, 2018).

Some of the more popular theories, like the scapegoat theory, fail when held to the scrutiny of Scripture, and they also distort the nature of the Gospel itself. Take Derek Prince's explanation, for instance: "Here is the true meaning and purpose of the cross. On it, a divinely ordained exchange took place. First, Jesus endured in our place all the evil consequences that were due by divine justice to our iniquity. Now, in exchange, God offers us all the good that was due to the sinless obedience of Jesus."[18] At first glance, this is an innocuous enough statement and appears to be strongly protestant. However, noticing that he explains God "offers us all the good…" is a small distortion that takes away from the work of the cross. God does not merely *offer* us grace; He gives us grace. The exchange is beyond wiping our slate clean, but it is replacing it with untold riches and grace earned by Jesus Christ. The scapegoat theory fails because it does not finish the work by guaranteeing us the eternal riches and glory found only in Christ.

The correct answer is revealed to us through a combination of what we have seen. The clarity of the work of Jesus Christ is displayed in the NT work of the anonymously written book of Hebrews. The Epistle to the Hebrews, chapter 10, gives us a detailed account of the concept of Christ's sacrifice.

A Brief Exegesis of Hebrews 10:1-18

Hebrews 10:1-4

---

[18]   Derek Prince, *The Divine Exchange: The Sacrificial Death of Jesus Christ on the Cross* (Charlotte, NC: Derek Prince Ministries, 1995), 6.

The sacrificial system, as formally given, is said to be a σκιά, that is, a shadow of what is to come. The law, as given, was the shape cast by another object, not the object itself, but a shape of it. Even given in Leviticus, the sacrificial system was not to be the ultimate program put in place for the people of God, but rather something reminding them of a bigger and brighter object to come.

The criticism of this shadow of the law is in the statement that, "if these sacrifices had finally perfected the conscience of worshipers, they would have ceased—there would no longer be a need for them. Nevertheless, the opposite is the case: their continued performance serves as a "reminder" (*anamnēsis*) of sins, year by year (10:3).[19] Their ongoing necessity proves their ultimate uselessness.

Hebrews 10:5-10

---

[19] Luke Timothy Johnson, *Hebrews: A Commentary*, ed. C. Clifton Black, M. Eugene Boring, and John T. Carroll, 1st ed., The New Testament Library (Louisville, KY: Westminster John Knox Press, 2012), 249.

Recalling our earlier discussion on the issue of Cain and Abel's sacrifice, it is not that atonement comes in the sacrifice of animals, as the author of Hebrews points to the OT verses where God rejects these means as a final payment for what is needed, but instead requires perfection in human form, namely the form of Christ. "It is only when Christ offers himself as the final sacrifice for sins that atonement is achieved."[20] Not only this, but Allen indicates that verse 7 is evidence that Christ regarded himself as fulfilling the prophecy of Scripture, which is a further refutation to AQ, as while Isaac may have been actively involved, according to some Jewish scholars, there is no possible way he could have known the mind of God the way, Christ did, or saw himself as a potential atonement to His people. Some may argue with the accuracy of this statement, but the servant aspect of this passage and Christ's understanding of His purpose and Isaac, with his potential purpose, is not equal. Abraham himself had confidence that God *could* raise Isaac from the dead, but Christ *knew* His Father would act on His behalf and was acutely aware that His Father's will was at work (Jn 16:16-22).

Perhaps it is here in Hebrews 10:5 that Modéus also considers, as he earlier illustrated for us, the cultic sense of the act of sacrifice. "The word "offering" (προσφορά) is used rarely in the LXX, but a little more frequently in the NT, and when used exclusively for an offering in the cultic sense."[21]

---

[20]   David L. Allen, Hebrews, The New American Commentary (Nashville, TN: B & H Publishing Group, 2010), 497.

[21]   David L. Hicks, "Significant Silence: Christ's Death as Sacrifice and the "Implied Reader" in Paul's Letter to the Galatians." Order No. 10133846, Westminster Theological Seminary, 2016. In PROQUESTMS ProQuest Central; ProQuest Central; ProQuest Dissertations & Theses Global.

        While a passage like this undoubtedly strengthens his argument of sacrifice pointing back to the cause of the action, rather than the action itself, he still ultimately fails. A unique premise given to the reader is that the actions of ritual sacrifice as born by the necessity of man to create acts to represent causes. However, the act of death on a cross is an idea born in the mind of God, and far from the inclinations of man (Rom 5:7).

Hebrews 10:11-18

        The key verse of this entire pericope lay within these final verses. The author describes to us the daily work of OT priests, ministering, and continually offering sacrifice for that which can never be satisfied. The exhaustion and fatigue are here felt in the language of the author—acting upon something that, in its essence, cannot be satisfied by the action taken upon it. The illustration is like a firefighter never able to quench a raging fire but knowing that merely giving up would result in unfathomable destruction.

        Christian A. Eberhart elaborates on this passage by asking if Jesus can historically be said to be "a priest"? He alludes that the Gospels do not describe Christ in this manner,[22] yet this understanding of His person and work is critical to our understanding of both sacrifice and atonement.

        Eberhart gives the scholar a sigh of relief in noting that in connecting Hebrews 9 to Hebrews 10, it is clear that the author is not trying to make a historical connection, but instead is using a metaphor in regarding Christ as a priest to give us insight into a divine mystery, and without such a metaphor, we would struggle to understand such a concept.[23]

---

[22]   Eberhart, Christian A. and Donald Schweitzer. "The Unique Sacrifice of Christ According to Hebrews 9: A Study in Theological Creativity." Religions 10, no.1(2019):47, http://ezproxy.liberty.edu/login?url=https://searchproquest.com.ezproxy.l iberty.edu/docview/2326927948?accountid=12085.

However, the life of the passage is verse 14. It is by one προσφορά that we have been τελειόω. This sacrifice has *perfected* Christians. This perfection is the essence of all we have reviewed. In seeking an understanding of how the death of Christ fits into a synthesized understanding of both concepts of *sacrifice* and *ritual*, we find harmony.

Sacrificially, an act to satisfy the necessity of atonement and worship has been given. However, it is a far cry from the sacrifice of an animal or grain or vegetation. This sacrifice is a sacrifice of such a high price that it is not of our world, but rather enjoining itself to our race to save it from the consequences of its actions. The sacrifice, which is typically to be of something of value to man, instead is of value to the offended party, given on behalf of the offender, to appease His own need for perfection, and a requirement to maintain His own character of holiness in the face of His creation's rebellion.

Ritualistically, this hits the notes of Modéus' core concept, that we need terminology that better helps us look at the cause of the sacrifice. Because the sacrifice is Jesus Christ, we do not want to turn away from the object of sacrifice in favor of the cause, interminably. However, we equally must recall the *reason* for such a valuable sacrifice to be made.

---

[23]   Ibid.

The author of Hebrews helps us understand both cause and object in verse 14, by declaring to us that Christ, as an object of infinite value, was necessary to satisfy a cause of cosmic proportions. What priests could not do for decades; Christ did with *one single sacrifice.* Christ settled the debt with God. However, He does more than this— Christ also *perfects* those whom God called to be His own. The sacrificial system, working day and night, could only temporarily expiate the sin of the people even though it is always looking back to the offense; but it could never *perfect* them—this was only possible in the object of Christ.

What This Means for Practical Theology

For Practical Theology, this is a picture of what has and will continue to separate God from the other cults of the past, present, and future. While the OT & NT believers alike undeniably share ritualistic tendencies with nations around them, our differentiation is in both the cause and object of our worship.

In our apologetic of the Scripture, a popular rebuttal from secularists and idolaters alike is that the OT sacrificial system is structured like that of many other groups. However, none of those groups can point to the cause of their sacrificial system and declare it only a shadow of an object to come, and that their god provides that on their behalf. This is unique to Christianity.

Through such an atonement, the Christian finds justification, not in works and obeisance, but in unmerited favor given directly from the hand of God at His own cost. Justification is overlooked in connection to atonement, but it is the result of cause and object, considered together. Robert Letham brings clarity to this by saying, "The death of the cross was not the end for Jesus. Indeed, it would have been a tragic charade if the empty tomb had not followed. In turn, it was the resurrection that gave meaning to the death and cast light for the disciples on all that had gone before."[24]

So, for our day to day theology, for something the lay Christian can grab hold of, the typical Christian conception of this topic should bring confidence upon our lives. God has made a practical mockery of cultic ritual and surpassed the expectation of a sacrificial system. God has fundamentally evidenced Himself as the God of power, justice, and mercy.

How This Builds the Church

Practically, what this means is that the Church needs a broader view on the death of Christ in consideration of the context of sacrifice. There tends to be an overemphasis on the cause or the object, depending upon denominational affiliation.

The Psalmist declares, in the 105th chapter, that Israel is to recall the works of the Lord on their behalf; this was the proposed response to considering the object of their praise. Beyond a focus on just the existence of God, which is undoubtedly a glorious thing, they are to recall the reason why they can attribute the worship of Divinity to Him. Surely, there would be other gods that would come along and try to gain their affection through immediacy. However, the keys to steadfast strength are built into works that God has already done as well, and what offense has been forgiven as well. It is not just man's sin against man, but his consistent internal war with God that is in view.

Conclusion

---

[24] Robert Letham, *The Work of Christ*, ed. Gerald Bray, Contours of Christian Theology (Downers Grove, IL: InterVarsity Press, 1993), 178–179.

Having built a better framework for emphasis on the concept of the death of Jesus Christ, by investigating the common understanding of sacrifice, this author has presented no new theories on atonement or no new revelations on the person and work of Jesus Christ. Instead, and rightly, I have sought to turn the Christian back to the best and more accurate way of looking at what God initially instituted, why He instituted it, and what it ultimately was designed to do.

It is commonplace in the Church that heresies will arise as days go on, and these are, to be sure, works of the flesh[25] and Tom Ascol notes, in a discussion about how to approach heresy, "The refusal to acknowledge its existence and to renounce it in clear terms is a denial of the faith once delivered to the saints. Genuine confession of faith always consists of both an affirmation of saving truth and a denial of that which opposes saving truth."[26]

Some may argue that the cause of sacrifice is seen in the infinite worth of the object, Jesus Christ. However, this author would point out that recent damnable heresies that have slowly crept into the visible Church include, but are not limited to denial of original sin, rejection of the divinity of Christ, refutation on the nature of the atonement, and a modern evangelical dependence upon the doctrine of semi-Pelagianism. All of these could be severely hindered or eliminated with a sound understanding of both the cause and object in the concept of sacrifice and death of Christ.

---

[25]   Allen C. Myers, The Eerdmans Bible Dictionary (Grand Rapids, MI: Eerdmans, 1987), 481.

[26]   Tom Ascol, "When We Talk about Heresy, Let's Be Honest," *The Founders Journal: When We Talk about Heresy, Let's Be Honest, Winter*, no. 27 (1997): 9.

It will be the responsibility of the faithful biblical scholars and exegetes of the sacred text to uphold the full, detailed truth which is left for us in the Bible, and as faithful men of truth, teach others who will be faithful to pass it on. This responsibility should be the burden of those called to scholarship and service in the edification of the Church of Jesus Christ.

Bibliography

Allen C. Myers, The Eerdmans Bible Dictionary (Grand Rapids, MI: Eerdmans, 1987).

Abraham Oh, "Canonical understanding of the sacrifice of Isaac: The influence of the Jewish tradition." HTS Teologiese Studies 72, no. 3 (2016): 1+. Gale Academic OneFile (accessed May 23, 2020).

David L. Allen, *Hebrews*, The New American
Commentary (Nashville, TN: B & H
Publishing Group, 2010).

David L. Hicks, "Significant Silence: Christ's
Death as Sacrifice and the "Implied
Reader" in Paul's Letter to the Galatians."
Order No. 10133846, Westminster
Theological Seminary, 2016. In
PROQUESTMS ProQuest Central;
ProQuest Central; ProQuest Dissertations &
Theses Global.

Derek Kidner, Genesis: An Introduction and
Commentary, vol. 1, Tyndale Old
Testament Commentaries (Downers Grove,
IL: InterVarsity Press, 1967).

Derek Prince, *The Divine Exchange: The Sacrificial
Death of Jesus Christ on the Cross*
(Charlotte, NC: Derek Prince Ministries,
1995).

Douglas Stuart, *Hosea–Jonah*, vol. 31, Word
Biblical Commentary (Dallas: Word,
Incorporated, 1987).

Eberhart, Christian A. and Donald Schweitzer. "The
Unique Sacrifice of Christ According to
Hebrews 9: A Study in Theological
Creativity." Religions 10, no. 1 (2019): 47,
**http://ezproxy.liberty.edu/login?url=http
s://searchproquest.com.ezproxy.liberty.e
du/docview/2326927948?accountid=1208
5**

F. L. Cross and Elizabeth A. Livingstone, eds., The
Oxford Dictionary of the Christian Church
(Oxford; New York: Oxford University
Press, 2005).

Iain D. Campbell, *Opening up Exodus*, Opening Up
Commentary (Leominster: Day One
Publications, 2006).

James W. Watts, "Review of Sacrifice and Symbol: Biblical Šĕlāmîm in a Ritual Perspective by Modéus, Martin." Review of Biblical Literature (2006).

Lesley Difransico, "Sacrifice," ed. Douglas Mangum et al., *Lexham Theological Wordbook*, Lexham Bible Reference Series (Bellingham, WA: Lexham Press, 2014).

Luke Timothy Johnson, *Hebrews: A Commentary*, ed. C. Clifton Black, M. Eugene Boring, and John T. Carroll, 1st ed., The New Testament Library (Louisville, KY: Westminster John Knox Press, 2012).

Mark Olivero, "Theories of Atonement," in Lexham Survey of Theology, ed. Mark Ward et al. (Bellingham, WA: Lexham Press, 2018).

Millard J. Erickson, Christian Theology, 3rd ed. (Grand Rapids, MI: Baker Academic, 2013).

O'Leary, Joseph. "Five Books on Sacrifice: New Approaches in Sacrifice Studies." Reviews in religion and theology 21, no. 3 (July 2014).

R. K. Harrison, *Jeremiah and Lamentations: An Introduction and Commentary*, vol. 21, Tyndale Old Testament Commentaries (Downers Grove, IL: InterVarsity Press, 1973).

Robert Letham, *The Work of Christ*, ed. Gerald Bray, Contours of Christian Theology (Downers Grove, IL: InterVarsity Press, 1993).

T. Seidl, "שְׁלָמִים," ed. G. Johannes Botterweck, Helmer Ringgren, and Heinz-Josef Fabry, trans. David E. Green, Theological Dictionary of the Old Testament (Grand Rapids, MI; Cambridge, U.K.: William B. Eerdmans Publishing Company, 2006).

Tom Ascol, "When We Talk about Heresy, Let's Be Honest," *The Founders Journal: When We Talk about Heresy, Let's Be Honest, Winter*, no. 27 (1997).

Christopher N. Croom is a Christian, Husband, and Father. Chris is also the founder of CROSS & Culture, a network of social media pages, including Facebook, Twitter, Parler, and YouTube. In his spare time, he is also a youth basketball coach.

Chris obtained his Master's Degree in Bible Exposition from Liberty University and is a current Doctoral student in the Bible Exposition program as well.

In the years to come, Chris looks forward to growing the CROSS & Culture brand, which desires to help Christians engage the world around them, by renewing a sense of theology, philosophy, logic, and apologetic within the Church, that they can seek the elect of Christ.